Individual Counseling
Activities for Children
(Grades K-6)

By Robert P. Bowman, Ph.D.
&
Susan C. Bowman, Ed.S., L.P.C.

youth light
inc.

Post Office Box 115
Chapin, South Carolina 29036
(800) 209-9774 (803) 345-1070
Fax (803) 345-0888
yl@sc.rr.com
www.YouthLight.com

Cover Design by Elizabeth Madden
Illustrations by Walt Lardner
Project Layout by Melissa Hare
Reprint by Tonya Daugherty

ISBN 1-889636-12-6

Library of Congress 98-061124

10 9 8 7 6 5 4 3
Printed in the United States of America

This material has been adapted from
Becoming a Co-Pilot: A Handbook for Mentors of Children
by Robert P. Bowman, Ph.D. & Susan C. Bowman, Ed.S., L.P.C. ©1997

Introduction

This book is intended to help you build your collection of creative approaches for providing developmental counseling with children.

On the following pages, you will find 85 activities that you can use during your individual counseling sessions with children. These activities were designed around 11 developmental guidance topics or lessons.

How To Use This Book

In particular, this book may be useful in the following ways:

1. It can be used as a needs assessment tool. Children can look through the topics with you and select one or more on which to begin exploring. In this way, the book helps you and the child to identify a place to start.

2. It can provide a catalyst that can help you and a child approach a topic that might be emotionally sensitive to him/her. It may be more comfortable for a child to begin sharing personal information about such a topic if it were introduced through a story, or an activity, rather than through direct questioning.

3. It can be a valuable information resource on a variety of topics that are personalized for the developmental levels of elementary school students. It contains specific considerations, strategies, and hints that can help children explore and set new goals for themselves.

4. It can help individual counseling become more comprehensive and developmental in nature. The eleven lessons contained in this book cover a wide range of guidance topics designed to help children increase their coping competencies.

5. It can add to your collection of fun, engaging activities that you can use in your one-to-one counseling sessions with children. It can also provide you with ideas that you may find useful in some of your small group counseling and large group guidance sessions.

Recommendations for Using This Book

1. Have your student look through the eleven topics with you. Then, together, select the one(s) that seem most relevant or urgent to deal with first.

2. If the child has the ability, encourage him/her to read some of the activities along with you. Occasionally stop to make sure that the child understands what you are reading. Once you have read over an activity, discuss the information together.

3. Activities in each of the 11 lessons provide opportunities for you and the student to share your feelings, beliefs, and ideas on a variety of important issues. Be open and honest with your views while being a good listener as the child expresses his/her opinions.

4. Use these lessons occasionally, not during every meeting. Remember that these lessons should not become the primary work you do with your student. They intended to help you both focus on some important aspect of personal development. Instead, use the activities to help start discussions on the topics. Then, encourage the child to explore how the information relates to him/herself.

5. Don't worry too much about the sequence in which you cover these lessons with the child. Either of you may select lessons that seem most interesting or relevant.

6. Some of these lessons can be covered in one meeting while others may take extra time. Don't hesitate to stop and "capture the opportunity" if the child gets off the topic into something personally relevant.

7. The child may want to include some of the products of these activities in a "Personal Portfolio" that you can help him/her develop.

8. Once your student has worked through some of the lessons, encourage him/her to work with a younger student on the same lesson(s). With your encouragement and guidance, this can be an extremely rewarding experience for the student.

Table of Contents

LESSON 1: "MY ABILITIES"

Helping a child feel lovable and capable are two important goals of counseling children. One way to approach this is to determine some of the abilities the student has, then to provide continuing affirmations of these abilities to him/her.

A. Identifying Abilities

Every child has a unique combination of personal strengths or abilities. To identify these, you might interview the child's teacher, parents, mentor, peers, or others who might know him/her. Try to determine at least five special abilities your student has and write them down. Ask your student to tell you what he/she can do well, and add these words to your list. As you become familiar with your student, you might notice other abilities that you want to add to your list.

Activity 1: Use the "Ability Words Checklist"
Grades K-5
Materials: A copy of the following "Ability Words"

The following list of "Ability Words" can help you find the best terms to describe your student. As you discover new words that may apply to your student, place a check next to them on the list, or write them on this page. Note that even though some of these words may be beyond the vocabulary of your child, he/she may enjoy learning them anyway. Help your student learn his/her own list of ability words. Note that for students in grades K-2, look over this list in advance to identify which words might be most appropriate for their vocabulary level.

Ability Words

❑ Adventurous
❑ Appreciative
❑ Artistic
❑ Athletic
❑ Brave
❑ Bright
❑ Calm
❑ Caring
❑ Careful
❑ Cooperative
❑ Creative
❑ Curious
❑ Dependable

❑ Determined
❑ Eager
❑ Energetic
❑ Fair
❑ Faithful
❑ Flexible
❑ Forgiving
❑ Friendly
❑ Funny
❑ Generous
❑ Gentle
❑ Giving
❑ Good Sport

❑ Hard Worker
❑ Helpful
❑ Honest
❑ Leader
❑ Loving
❑ Loyal
❑ Motivated
❑ Neat
❑ Open-Minded
❑ Organized
❑ Patient
❑ Positive
❑ Prepared

❑ Resourceful
❑ Respectful
❑ Sensitive
❑ Sharing
❑ Thoughtful
❑ Trustworthy
❑ Unselfish

B. Affirming Abilities

Once a few words have been identified to describe some of your student's abilities, use one or more of the following strategies. These suggestions will provide you with different ways to make affirmations to your student. They will also help the student learn to use self-talk to affirm him/herself.

Activity 2: Make an "I Can"

Grades K-5

Materials: Empty soup can, magazines/newspapers, two pairs of scissors, glue/paste.

An "I Can" is an emptied soup-sized can with one end open. Work with your student to cut out as many pictures of large eyes as you can. Don't cut just around the outlines of the eyes, cut a larger circle around each. Sometimes, cut both eyes out in one piece. Note that animal and cartoon eyes can be included and will add more variety to the look of the can.

With your student, paste the pictures around the can until it is covered with the eyes. Now you have a can coated with eyes—an "I Can." When finished, you and your student should partially fill the can with small objects or pictures of things that represent his/her unique combination of abilities. You may also look for ability words in magazines, cut them out, and place them in the can. Later, you or your student might empty out the contents of the can on a table and review the collection of his/her ability words and symbols. Other times, you and your student might look in the can for one or two particular abilities that might help him/her to have more confidence in a certain situation.

Activity 3: Make an "Ability Bag"

Grades K-5

Materials: Paper bag, magazines/newspapers, two pairs of scissors, glue/paste.

Similar to the "I Can," an ability bag will contain objects, pictures, and words that describe the child's abilities. The bag has the advantage of being larger, so it can hold larger objects. Almost any size paper bag will work. The bag can also be drawn on or decorated by the child. His/her name may be colored or painted on it. Look through magazines and/or newspapers with the student and paste on pictures that describe him/her. You might suggest how some pictures remind you of the child, but give him/her the final decision as to what is pasted on the bag.

Activity 4: Play "Toilet Paper Brainstorm"

Grades K-5

Materials: One roll of toilet paper.

Have the child unwind some toilet paper from a roll. Then, have him/her tear off individual sections of the paper he/she has taken from the roll. Each time a section is torn off, the child should tell about one of his/her abilities by completing the sentence, "I can . . . ."

Activity 5: Sing the "Ability Song"

Grades K-2
Materials: None

The Ability Song consists of made-up lyrics that describe the child's particular abilities. It follows the tune of "Are You Sleeping." Use the following example to help you develop your song. Note that the song can be repeated for most, or all of his/her ability words. You might want to write the lyrics down for future reference.

"I know Jennifer."	*Child echoes*
"She is friendly."	*Child echoes*
"It's easy to like her."	*Child echoes*
"She has a big smile."	*Child echoes*

Activity 6: Play "Show Me Your Ability"

Grades K-5
Materials: None

Once you know some words that identify the child's abilities, think of some ways he/she might be able to demonstrate each ability to you through play. As the child shows you an ability, say something like, "Wow! You sure are showing your _____ (ability word)." The following are some examples of ways he/she could show your abilities through play:

Ability	**Have the child:**
Adventurous:	Be the leader while taking you for a walk.
Brave:	Perform in a play or skit.
Caring:	Make a gift for another person.
Creative:	Draw/paint a picture, or make up a story/rap song.
Friendly:	Introduce you to one of his/her friends.
Funny:	Tell you a funny story or joke.
Helpful:	Assist someone while you watch.
Organized:	Show you his/her desk, locker, or notebook.
Sensitive:	Put on two puppets and make up a story showing how one understands the feelings of the other.
Trustworthy:	Cover your eyes with your hands and allow the child to take you for a short "blind" walk.

Other Activities

Activity 7 *(Grades K-5):* Take a walk around the school with the child to meet some of the people who know him/her. Ask them to tell you about the child's abilities in front of him/her. You might want to talk with these people before bringing the child to them. Let them know some of the ability words you have identified for the child and ask them if they have any others to add to your list.

Activity 8 *(Grades K-5):* Find one or more stories that provide examples of abilities which your student possesses. If the child can't read yet, read the stories to him/her. Otherwise, read the stories together. Explore how the stories relate to the child's abilities.

Activity 9 *(Grades K-5):* Identify one or more careers in which the child's abilities are valued. Then, take the child to see the people working in that field. Emphasize how your student's abilities would be helpful in the job. If taking a trip to a job site is not possible, conduct a phone interview, read about the career in a book, or use the internet to search for relevant information.

LESSON 2: "MY ATTITUDE"

Children's attitudes reflect how they view themselves. When a child has low self-esteem, he/she will likely have a negative attitude toward others. For example, children with low self-esteem may make very negative comments about their teachers, family members, and peers.

Helping a child change his/her attitude is not easy. One might begin by teaching children what the term "attitude" means and how positive and negative attitudes differ from each other. Then, they might benefit from exploring and practicing different situations in which they can change their attitudes from negative to positive.

Activity 10: Understanding Negative and Positive Attitudes

Grades K-5
Materials: None

Read the following four situations, one at a time, to the child. Have him/her show a frown each time he/she hears a "negative attitude" and a smile each time he/she hears a "positive attitude." When you have completed the list, make up other situations and have the child respond to each with a smile or frown, or with the words "positive attitude" or "negative attitude." Afterwards, have the child describe some situations to you while you frown, smile, or guess which kind of attitude he/she is describing.

- A boy gets into trouble with the teacher and throws his books on the floor.
- A girl walks up to a new student in school and asks if she wants to play with her.
- A girl tells her friends that she is not going to play with them anymore.
- A boy gets a low grade on a test, but says he's going to work hard to do better on the next test.

Activity 11: Wear "Attitude Glasses"*

Grades K-5
Materials: One pair of Sunglasses

Tell the child that a positive attitude is like putting on "rose-colored glasses." Pull out a pair of sunglasses. Explain that when things are upsetting to you, you can look at these things differently and find something positive about them. Show the child how someone can change a negative attitude into a positive one by telling the following situations while you either wear or don't wear the glasses.

Glasses off: "I really hate this school and everyone in it!"
Glasses on: "I get upset sometimes at school, but I like it when my
                  teacher says something nice to me."

Glasses off: "No one in this school wants to be my friend."
Glasses on: "I need to do more things that will help others see me
                  as a friendly person."

Glasses off: "I'll never do well in my schoolwork. I'm just a loser!"
Glasses on: "No matter what has happened in the past, I know that I
                  can be a winner in school!"

* Adapted from an activity developed by Dr. Linda Myrick, Adjunct Professor, University of Florida.

Activity 12: Make an "Attitude Collage"
Grades K-5
Materials: Construction paper, magazines/newspapers, two pairs of scissors, glue/paste.

Place two pieces of construction paper on the table. Title one, "Positive Attitudes" and the other "Negative Attitudes." Work together with the child to cut out pictures from magazines and/or newspapers of people who look like they have positive or negative attitudes. Positive attitude pictures are pasted on one collage, while negative attitude pictures are pasted on the other. Then talk about the difference between the two collages.

Activity 13: Change a Puppet's Attitude
Grades K-3
Materials: At least two hand puppets.

Have the child choose two puppets, one for him/herself and the other for you to put on your hand. Make up a story in which your puppet has a negative attitude toward someone or something. Perhaps use one or more of the "Glasses Off" situations from Activity 11. Ask the child's puppet to say or do something that will help your puppet have a more positive attitude about the situation.

Activity 14: Draw the Attitudes
Grades K-5
Materials: Crayons, drawing paper.

Have the child use crayons to make two drawings about situations he/she has seen in school. The first drawing should show someone with a positive attitude and the second, someone with a negative attitude. Ask the child to tell you about what happened in each situation.

Another drawing could be of a cartoon character with a positive attitude and another with a negative attitude. Then, have the child tell you his/her story about the characters' attitudes. Ask him/her how the negative character could be helped to have a more positive attitude.

Activity 15: Show Thumbs-Up or Thumbs-Down

Grades K-5
Materials: None

Read each of the following items to the child and add more of your own if you wish. Ask the child to give a thumbs-up or thumbs-down to each. Thumbs-up means that he/she has a positive attitude toward it, whereas thumbs-down means that he/she has a negative attitude toward it. Record the child's answers by placing an up or down arrow in the space before each item.

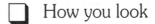

▲ = Positive Attitude   ▼ = Negative Attitude

- [ ] Your school
- [ ] How you look
- [ ] Your voice
- [ ] Your dreams (hopes)
- [ ] Your teacher
- [ ] School lunch
- [ ] Getting up in the morning
- [ ] Going home after school
- [ ] Playing with your friends
- [ ] Taking a test in school
- [ ] How you are dressed
- [ ] Thinking about what will happen to you next year

Other Activities

Activity 16 *(Grades K-5):* Have the child identify stories about characters with negative or positive attitudes. You might also identify other stories that show attitudes and read them to him/her.

Activity 17 *(Grades K-5):* Have the child tell, write, draw, or act out something he/she did that day that showed a negative or positive attitude.

Activity 18 *(Grades K-5):* When you notice the child having a negative attitude, help him/her see the situation from a positive perspective.

LESSON 3: "MY FEELINGS"

"Feelings aren't good or bad, they just are." This statement holds a lot of wisdom for people of all ages. Unfortunately, many children are taught that some feelings are "good" or "positive" while other feelings are "bad" or "negative." As a result, some children develop the belief that some feelings are bad or wrong to have. They become discouraged from feeling angry, sad, or scared. Some little boys, for example, are discouraged by their families and/or classmates from crying or showing that they are afraid. They are told, "Men don't cry" or "Don't be a cry baby." Little girls, on the other hand, are sometimes discouraged from admitting or showing angry feelings. They are told, "That's not nice. You shouldn't feel that way about (him, her, or me)."

Boys and girls should learn that it is alright to feel sad, scared, or angry. It's how someone **shows** these feelings that may be okay or not okay. For example, it is alright for someone to feel angry, but there are right and wrong ways to express this feeling. The following activities will help your young student learn about feelings. They will also encourage the child to tell you more about his or her feelings with you.

Activity 19: *Name the Animal's Feeling*

Grades K-3
Materials: One or more stuffed animals or hand puppets.

Hold the stuffed animal or puppet and have it tell the child about an emotional situation, then ask him/her to guess the feelings. The following are some examples of situations:

- A pig doesn't think that other animals understand that it is actually very smart and clean, too. (sad, lonely, not liked)

- A turtle just won a race. (happy, proud, excited)

- A lion is shaking because it knows that hunters are nearby. (scared, worried, afraid)

- A dog is lying on the floor, wagging its tail when it sees you. (friendly, happy, excited)

- A mother alligator is upset because someone is getting too close to the eggs in her nest. (angry, mad, worried)

- A cat is purring and rubbing against your legs. (happy, loving, content)

Activity 20: *Drawing Me With Happy and Upset Feelings*

Grades K-5
Materials: Crayons and drawing paper.

Have the child draw him/herself being "happy" on one piece of paper, and "upset" on another piece of paper. Then, ask him/her questions such as:

- How would someone know by looking at your picture, if you were having happy (or upset) feelings?

- What is something that makes you feel as happy (upset) as you appear to be in your picture?

Activity 21: Sing (or Rap) a Song about Feelings

Grades K-5
Materials: One copy of the song.

I Have Lots of Feelings and They're Okay *

I have lots of feelings and they're okay.
They jump up inside me every day.
If I was the President, I would say,
I have lots of feelings and they're okay.

I feel happy when I'm with my friends,
And I feel happy when the school day ends.
And I feel happy when I get to play,
'Cause happy is a feeling and it's okay.

I feel sad when I say good-bye,
And I feel sad when a bird can't fly.
And I feel sad when it rains all day,
But sad is a feeling and it's okay.

I feel proud when I bake a cake,
And I feel proud of my new pet snake.
And I feel proud when I stand and say,
"Proud is a feeling and it's okay."

I feel scared when my snake gets out,
Mom doesn't know it yet, but she'll find out.
And when she does, maybe then I'll say,
(shout) "Mom, scared is a feeling and it's okay!"

I have lots of feelings and they're okay,
They jump up inside me every day.
If I was the President, I would say,
I have lots of feelings and they're okay.

* Lyrics and music by Robert P. Bowman, Copyright, 1997 (Copied with permission)

Activity 22: Point to the Feeling Faces

Grades K-5
Materials: One copy of the "Feeling Faces."

Show the feeling faces on this page to the child and ask him/her to point to the face that best shows how he/she would feel in each of the following situations. Brainstorm words that describe each feeling.

1. Someone is telling lies about you.

2. Your teacher tells you that you did a good job on your school work.

3. A dog that you don't know begins growling at you.

4. You are leaving your home in the morning to go to school.

5. You are leaving school to go back home.

6. Someone steals your dessert.

7. It's time for lunch.

8. Someone tells you that they want to beat you up.

9. Someone asks you to play with them.

10. You see an animal that is hurt.

Feeling Faces

Other Activities

Activity 23: *(Grades K-5):* Ask the child to find books or magazines in the school media center that show different feelings. Read the stories to the child or have him/her read them to you. Identify the different feelings as you read along.

Activity 24: *(Grades K-5):* Ask the child to look in a mirror. As you name different feelings, have him/her practice showing each with his/her face.

Activity 25: *(Grades K-5):* Provide some crayons and drawing paper for the child. Then ask him/her to draw designs to show the following feelings, with one feeling shown on each page.

- Happy
- Angry
- Peaceful

- Sad
- Excited
- Scared

LESSON 4: "MY ANGER"

Anger is one feeling that some children, adolescents, and adults don't handle very well. It is a secondary emotion that usually follows feelings of hurt or frustration. Children can benefit by learning about anger and nonviolent strategies that they can use when they become angry. Ask your student to tell about what each of the following children are doing to "let their anger out."

Activity 26: How "Hot" do I Get?

Grades K-5

Materials: One copy of the "Anger Thermometers" and a red crayon, magic marker, pencil, or pen.

Show the child the empty "Anger Thermometers" below. Then read one of the following situations and ask him/her to color in the thermometer to show how angry he/she would become. Explain that more anger is "hotter" and should be shown with higher temperatures. For younger children you may have to show how to color the thermometers to show different temperatures. Repeat this activity for the five situations below.

How "hot" do you get when:
1. You get <u>blamed</u> for something you didn't do?
2. Someone doesn't keep their <u>promise</u> to you?
3. You can't find your <u>pencil</u>?
4. Someone laughs at you and calls you <u>names</u>?
5. Someone accidentally knocks you <u>down</u>?

Anger Thermometer

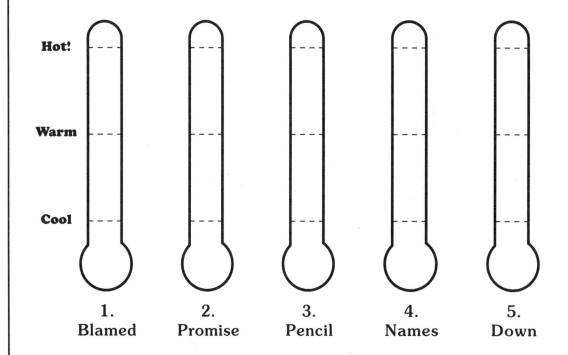

Activity 27: Things That "Bug" Me
Grades K-3
Materials: Clay or Play Doh®, glue or paste.

Have the child make three or four little bugs out of some form of modeling clay (or Play Doh®). When finished, place each bug at the top of a page of drawing paper. Then ask the child to draw on each page something that really bothers or "bugs" him/her. When finished, use glue to attach the bugs permanently to the pages.

An alternative way to do this activity is to have the child hold one of his/her clay bugs in one hand. While looking at this bug, the child should tell one thing that "bugs" him/her. When finished, the child is invited to smash the clay figure in his/her hand. Note that this alternative can be fun and cathartic for children.

Activity 28: Try to Get Out of This One
Grades K-5
Materials: One "Fingercuffs."

Purchase "Fingercuffs" which are sold in some amusement stores, though they are sometimes referred to by other names. Most people have seen Fingercuffs—they are like handcuffs for two of your fingers. A Fingercuff is a woven tube that, when a finger is placed in each end, will resist letting you pull your fingers back out. The solution is to push the fingers closer together to make the tube expand slightly in diameter. Then, the fingers can be removed easily.

Help the child see that this is like anger. When you become very upset, it is best to try to relax before trying to work out the situation.

Activity 29: *Practice Letting My Anger Out*

Grades K-5

Materials: *One wadded up piece of paper, clay or Play Doh®, and/or small soft ball.*

Disclose to the child some of the positive ways you let your anger out. Then, have him/her practice some of the following strategies:

☛ Squeeze something like a ball of wadded up paper, clay like material, or a very soft ball.

☛ Press your hands tightly together.

☛ Say to yourself over and over again, "I can be calm."

☛ Take two slow deep breaths.

☛ Count to ten before doing anything.

☛ Walk away and then think about something good you can do.

☛ Talk with someone about what made you so mad.

☛ Exercise, if possible.

Activity 30: Don't Let Your Anger Blow Up

Grades K-5

Materials: One deflated balloon.

Explain to the child that when a student is sleeping in the morning, he/she is relaxed and not experiencing anger. Suddenly, the alarm goes off and the student's anger may start (blow a little into the balloon). Then, someone in the family yells at the student for not getting out of bed right away (inflate the balloon a little more). Next, the student misses the school bus and gets wet because it starts to rain (inflate more). Then, when the student gets to school, the teacher becomes upset because the student is tardy again (inflate more). During lunch, they serve the student's least favorite meal, boiled turkey gizzards (inflate more). Then hold the balloon so no air escapes and stop the activity.

Ask the child to tell you what is eventually going to happen with the balloon if you keep adding more air. Then ask, how this is like someone who becomes more and more angry.

Ask the child what the student in the story could have done to let some of the anger out, without hurting anyone. Read the following list of possibilities with the child and ask whether it is a good or bad idea for the student to help let out his/her anger. After each good idea, release a little air out of the balloon to show that the idea helped to release pressure. After each bad idea blow air into the balloon.

What if the student:
- Started a fight?
- Breathed deeply and counted to ten?
- Kicked the wastepaper basket in the classroom?
- Talked with the teacher or school counselor about it?
- Talked with a friend about it?
- Yelled at the teacher?
- Remembered that he/she was really a good person?

Other Activities

Activity 31 *(Grades K-5):* Ask the child to compose a rap song with you about anger and its consequences. Then, record it and/or perform it for younger students.

Activity 32 *(Grades K-5):* Monitor the child's angry behavior by staying in close communication with his/her teacher, parent, and/or guardian. Set a goal with the child for improving his/her methods of coping with anger. Offer incentives to him/her for improvements.

Activity 33 *(Grades K-5):* Take a trip to a local martial arts program. In particular, seek a program that features violence prevention and does not overemphasize competition.

LESSON 5: "MY FRIENDS"

Learning about how to start, sustain, and end friendships are important tasks for children to learn. Corporate personnel directors consistently agree that the most important ability new employees should possess is the capacity to relate positively with others. As young as possible, children should begin working on their social competencies. In mastering these competencies, they learn important life skills such as how to make new friends, work and play cooperatively with their peers, express their feelings and beliefs appropriately, listen accurately and sensitively to others, and cope with the loss of a friend.

Activity 34: What is a Friend?

Grades K-5
Materials: None

Ask the child some or all the following questions about friendship. As he/she answers each question, repeat back what was said to allow him/her to reflect on what they're expression was. When you have finished, share your own answers to some of the questions. Perhaps you can allow the child to interview you.

- Who is one of your friends? What do you like to do together?
- What do you look for in a friend?
- How do you make a new friend?
- If a new student came to your class and you wanted to be friends, what could you do?
- When did a friend make you mad? Scared?
- When have you had something funny happen with a friend?
- How can you show a pet that you are its friend?
- If you could have all the friends you wanted, how many would you have?
- When have you lost a friend? What happened? How did you finally get over it?

Activity 35: Who is Your Friend?

Grades K-5
Materials: None

Have the child introduce you to one of his/her friends. Talk or play with both children for awhile. Then, ask them each to answer some of the questions in the previous activity. You might ask them to answer some of the questions about each other.

When finished, have the two children show you or tell you about something they like to do together. Listen attentively and summarize for them some of the qualities of friendship that you are hearing or seeing between them.

Activity 36: Develop a "Special Handshake"
Grades K-5
Materials: None

Encourage the child to help you invent a handshake that is special between you. Keep it simple and have fun. This handshake can become your own special way to greet, congratulate, and say good-bye to one another. The following are some examples of secret handshakes children have developed with their counselors.

- **Handshake from the Heart**
  Grasp each other's hand and begin little pulse-like squeezes to simulate a heartbeat.

- **Handshake Earthquake**
  Grasp hands and shake with a slight rumble between your hands.

- **Street Shake**
  Develop a series of three or four different moves that involve different ways of touching each others hands. For example, touch index fingers, then the backs of each other's thumbs, then grab each other's thumb with a single shake. Perhaps end with a "high five." Your child will enjoy helping you invent this.

- **Handshake With Sound Effects**
  Invent some kind of sound that you each make while touching each others hands.

- **Finger Shake**
  Like with the "Street Shake," this one involves a series of different steps. But, the "Finger Shake" is done completely with different combinations of contacts between fingers.

Activity 37: Feel the Warmth of Friendship

Grades K-5
Materials: None

Place one of your hands in front of you at about shoulder level. Place your palm forward, and ask the child to place his/her palm facing yours, about 12 inches away. Tell the child that this game is called "Feeling the Warmth of Friendship." Each of you should stare at each other's face while moving your hand forward toward your partner's hand. Stop just before your hands touch. When your hand is about a half-inch away from the child's hand, you both should feel a sudden surge of warmth from each other.

Put your hands down and talk with the child about how a friendship can be similar to this feeling. Also, you can relate this activity to the phrase "reach out to someone in friendship." Discuss how both people must reach towards each other if a special, healthy friendship is to develop.

Activity 38: Hand Mirroring
Grades K-5
Materials: None

This activity teaches children about the nature of listening and talking with others in a friendly way. It is a good follow-up to the previous activity because it is also based on an interaction between you and the child using your hands.

Sit facing one another and place your hands in positions similar to the beginning of the activity "Feel the Warmth of Friendship." This time, place your hands about three inches from the child's hands. Then explain to the child that you are going to move your hands around and you want him/her to try to mirror or copy your hand movements with his/her hands. However, he/she should keep looking at your face during the activity, not at your hands.

Begin with slow, smooth hand movements, then increase the challenge with more animated, creative movements. Once finished, reverse roles and try to follow the child's hand movements.

Discuss with the child the importance of learning to lead and follow in a friendship. For example, there are times when you will want your friend to listen to you. So, you will take the lead and you will want your friend to follow what you say. On the other hand, when your friend has something to tell you, you should be a good listener and try to follow his/her lead.

In addition, ask the child where each of you were looking during the activity. The answer is, at the face of the other person. Explain that this is what you should be doing when your friend is telling you something. You should be a good listener and look into his/her face to show that you are paying attention and that you are interested in what your friend is saying.

Other Activities

Activity 39 *(Grades K-5):* Ask the child to draw a picture of the two of you working and/or playing together. You might help him/her develop a personal portfolio and paste or tape this picture in it.

Activity 40 *(Grades K-5):* Take photos of the child with a friend doing things together. Once the photos are developed, have the child paste or tape the photos in his/her personal portfolio.

Activity 41 *(Grades K-5):* Discuss about a time when the child felt like he/she lost a friend. Explore with him/her different ways people grieve and that during these times it is okay to have sad and hurt feelings for awhile. Explain that you have never really lost a friend because you can always bring them back in your thoughts.

LESSON 6: "MY CONFLICTS WITH OTHERS"

Having conflicts with others is an inevitable part of life. Unless you choose to live the remainder of your life as a hermit, you will have to face occasional disputes with other people. Our successes or failures in handling these disputes depend in part on our mastery of skills and techniques of conflict resolution.

Children begin learning how to deal with conflicts as soon as they begin interacting with other people. By the time they enter kindergarten, some children have much better abilities to handle conflicts than others. Elementary schools are offering increasing opportunities for children to learn and practice conflict resolution strategies.

Activity 42: Open My Fist!

Grades 2-5
Materials: None

Make a fist with one of your hands and hold it out in front of the child. Then invite him/her to try to get your hand open in 30 seconds. Most children will try, at first, to use force and try to pry your fingers open. However, this can be very difficult to do and usually doesn't succeed. The more force they apply to your hand, the tighter you will probably grip your fingers together.

Afterwards, talk with the child about what happened. Help him/her understand that when you are trying to get someone to do something, force doesn't usually work very well. For older students, you might draw a parallel between trying to force someone's hand open and trying to pressure someone to open up to your point of view.

Next, brainstorm with the child other methods that might have a better chance of opening your hand. The following are some examples:

- Asking politely (inviting)
- Tickling (using humor)
- Offering to shake hands (changing the topic)
- Offering an incentive (rewarding)

Allow the child to choose a method other than force to open your fist. Then allow this method to succeed as he/she tries it on you. Talk about how different methods can be more effective than force, when you want to try to work out a conflict with someone else.

Activity 43: Magnetic Fingers

Grades 2-5
Materials: None

In this activity have the child make a fist with each of his/her hands. Then, the two fists should be placed together, wrist-to-wrist with thumbs on the upper side of each hand. Ask the child to extend his/her two index fingers to point away from the body. Then, he/she should begin pressing these two fingers against each other tightly. After about 30 seconds of pressing, ask the child to slightly separate the two fingers by about one inch, while keeping the fists together.

Children are amazed to see that their two fingers seem to move back together slowly on their own, almost as if they had magnetic attraction. Teach the child that this is like a conflict between two people. During some conflicts, people keep trying to use force against each other. But, if they would each separate for awhile, relax and take some time to listen to each other, then they would find that their ideas might come together without force.

Activity 44: Sometimes, You Can't Take It Back

Grades K-5
Materials: One tube or pump of toothpaste and a piece of paper or cardboard.

Ask the child to squeeze or pump out a pile of toothpaste onto a piece of paper or cardboard. He/she will enjoy doing this, but will wonder why. Then, ask the child to try to put all that toothpaste back into the tube. He/she will have fun trying to do this, but will discover that this is impossible to accomplish.

Ask the child, "How is the toothpaste like words that you might say to others when you are angry, that you wish you hadn't said?" Explore how we sometimes might say things that we later wish we could take back, but can't. It is important, especially when you are upset with someone, to think about what you are going to say before you say it.

Activity 45: *Work Out the Conflict*

Grades K-5
Materials: None

Read the following situations one at a time to the child. Then, discuss different ways, positive and negative, that the people could try to work out the conflict.

Conflict 1: On their way to lunch, two students start arguing about who should be first in line.

Conflict 2: Carla and Jamie had been best friends. One day Jamie started playing with another girl and Carla felt left out. Carla became angry and started a fight with the other girl.

Conflict 3: Anthony came back to his class and found his new pencils missing. He blamed Cedrick for stealing them because of what some other students said. That afternoon, Anthony took something out of Cedrick's desk to get even.

Conflict 4: Cassandra was shy and did not have many friends. Two girls in her class picked on her every day. Cassandra told the teacher and the two girls were punished. After school, the two girls came up to her and told her that they were going to "get her" on the bus. Cassandra was too afraid to get on the bus.

Conflict 5: Pete wanted to use the classroom computer. Another student had been using it for a long time, and wouldn't let Pete have a turn. Pete became angry and turned off the computer, erasing what the student had been working on.

Conflict 6: Allison's sister kept wearing her clothes without asking her. This time, she took one of Allison's favorite shirts and accidentally ripped it.

Conflict 7: A group of boys met after school. One boy wanted the group to play basketball. Another boy wanted the group to go to his home to see his new video game. A third boy wanted the group to go with him to the store to steal something.

Other Activities

Activity 46 *(Grades 3-5):* Meet with other children. As a group, develop a skit about conflicts and conflict resolution. Present the skit in front of one or more classrooms in the school. After the skit, each player could lead a small group of other students in a discussion about positive ways of handling different conflicts.

Activity 47 *(Grades 3-5):* Encourage your child to become a member of the school's peer mediation program. If the school does not have such a program, consider starting one in your school.

Activity 48 *(Grades 3-5):* Interview several people about a time when each of them positively handled a conflict they had with another person. Be sure to interview a variety of people such as students, teachers, volunteers, the principal, parents, custodians, food service workers, community and/or a school secretary.

LESSON 7: "MY CONFIDENCE WITH SCHOOLWORK"

One factor that determines a child's ability to be successful with schoolwork is his/her self-confidence. Children who consistently do well in school have their self-confidence regularly reinforced. Children who consistently fail to succeed with their schoolwork eventually become discouraged and may come to believe that it is hopeless for them to be successful.

Children with low self-confidence need a lot of understanding and encouragement. They need someone to help them learn that, in spite of past failures, they will always retain the potential to succeed. As a counselor for these children, you can encourage them to realize that they have many personal strengths they can use to help them with their schoolwork. In addition, there are several easy-to-learn study tricks that can help them apply their strengths more effectively to their schoolwork.

Activity 49: Four Steps to Being a "Winner" in School *

Grades K-5
Materials: One copy of "Four Winning Steps"

Help your child learn that there are four steps to being a winner in school (see below and the next page). Then, encourage your child to show you how he/she can use each step with actual schoolwork.

1. "I can **be** a winner"　　　2. "I can **show** I'm a winner"

3. "I can **start** like a winner"　　4. "I can **finish** like a winner"

* From *Peer Pals* by Bowman and Chanaca (AGS, 1994).

Four Winning Steps

1. **"I can *be* a winner!"** You have to believe deep inside of yourself that you can feel good about your work in school.

2. **"I can *show* I'm a winner!"** You will need to show your teacher and other students that you are trying to do your very best with your schoolwork.

3. **"I can *start* like a winner!"** Learn how to get ready for your work.

4. **"I can *finish* like a winner!"** Learn how to "hang in there" and finish your work with your best effort.

Activity 50: Keys to Becoming a Confident Learner

Grades 3-5

Materials: One photocopy of "The Five Keys to Success" (on the next page).

Give the child a copy of the next page of this book. Explain that he/she should practice these keys with schoolwork. Help your child learn each key. Then have him/her bring you some current school work. Encourage the child to talk about how each key could be used with this schoolwork.

The Five Keys to Success

Key #1: **Set a few new goals at a time.** Make these goals easy to accomplish in a short amount of time.

Key #2: **Picture yourself being successful.** Picture in your mind what it will be like when you reach your goals. Remember to think of this picture whenever you begin to feel frustrated or discouraged.

Key #3: **Control your inner voice.** Unfortunately, we sometimes say things to ourselves that discourage us. Change these negative messages to more positive ones like the following:

<u>Negative Self-Messages</u>	<u>Positive Self-Messages</u>
"I just can't do this work."	"I can do this work."
"I will never be able to do this."	"I will be able to do this."
"I will never be good at this."	"I can keep improving."
"I know I'm going to fail this."	"I'm going to do my best."

Key #4: **Reward your accomplishments.** When you know you have reached a short-term goal, or when you know you have done your best, treat yourself to something special.

Key #5: **Encourage others.** You may notice someone else who becomes discouraged about school. When this happens, listen to his/her feelings. Then, offer some positive suggestions such as how he/she might find a tutor. When you help others learn to think more positively, it can have a positive effect on you too!

Activity 51: "How Confident Am I?"

Grades 4-5

Materials: One copy of "Study Habits and Skills Checklist."

Study Habits and Skills Checklist

Here is a list for you to look through and discuss with the child. Begin by reading through each item together. Then ask the child to rate him/herself on each item.

1 = Poor	3 = So-So	4 = Good
2 = Not So Good		5 = Excellent

Classroom Effectiveness

____ **Keep Good Attendance:** Missing too much school puts you behind in your work.

____ **Set High Goals:** Believe in your ability to keep improving in your work.

____ **Show a Winning Attitude:** Show your teacher and classmates that you are trying your best in your work.

____ **Listen Carefully:** Pay close attention to everything the teacher says.

____ **Take Good Notes:** Learn to write down what the teacher says.

Memorizing Facts

____ **Use Acronyms:** Take the first letter of each term you want to memorize. Then make a nonsense word out of it. Or, you could create a new sentence with the same first letters for each word. For example, to memorize our planets in order from the sun, you can use the following statement (the first letter of each word corresponds with the name of a planet). "My Very Excellent Mother Just Sat Upon Nine Pins" (Mercury, Venus, Earth, Mars, Jupiter, Saturn, Uranus, Neptune, and Pluto).

____ **Use "Rap":** Recite the terms, or words you are trying to memorize with a rap rhythm. This beat can help you memorize much faster.

Taking a Test*

_____ **Prepare:** Make sure you have enough time to study for the test. Sometimes it may help to have a study partner or team. Also, make sure you get enough rest and have a healthy breakfast before the test.

_____ **Reduce Stress:** Think of the test as a challenge. If you are worried, slow down. Take a few slow, deep breaths and make positive statements to yourself about how you are capable of succeeding on the test.

_____ **Become Motivated:** Remember that each test is important and don't quit trying. Give each question your best effort.

_____ **Be Test-Wise:** Know how to make a good guess and be careful not to go too slow or too fast.

Studying Effectively at Home

_____ **Manage Your Time:** Use your time wisely. Set a time to start working and stick with it, without having to be reminded by your parents.

_____ **Prevent Distractions:** You will accomplish more in less time if you do not have a television or phone nearby. Find a place to study that is private and comfortable. Some students find that soft music can help them block out distractions and concentrate better.

Using Resource People

_____ **Ask Your Teacher:** Don't be afraid to ask your teacher for assistance. It shows you care.

_____ **Ask Other School Resource Staff:** There are several people in your school who may help you if you ask.

_____ **Ask Other Students:** Other students may be very willing to help you or work with you. Perhaps you can form a study group.

_____ **Ask Your Family:** Don't forget that others in your family can be great resources.

_____ **Ask Other People:** There may be other people in your community who would be pleased to help you. Some communities have tutoring and other student assistance programs available.

* Adapted from *The Test Buster Pep Rally* by R. P. Bowman (Educational Media, 1987).

Follow-Up:
First look over all items that the child rated a "4" or "5" and recognize his/her strong points. Then look at the items the child rated a "1" or "2." Help him/her set goals to improve in these areas. Then assist the child in selecting an area you will begin working on together.

Other Activities

Activity 52 *(Grades 2-5):* If the child is old enough to be receiving homework assignments from school, help him/her make a "Schoolwork Survival Kit." Decorate a small box and fill it with items like scissors, pencils, pens, crayons, *etc.* Perhaps attach or insert a "Homework Plan" consisting of a commitment to the place(s) and times studying will take place.

Activity 53 *(Grades 2-5):* Form a "Parent Partnership." Work with your child's parent(s)/guardian(s) to help him/her develop or improve study habits at home. You can become a valuable reinforcer to the child when parents give you a positive report of his/her special accomplishments. You might develop a "Homework Coupon" to give to your Child. After your Child earns five coupons, you might take him/her for breakfast or give a small token gift.

Activity 54 *(Grades 2-5):* Help the child find a "study buddy" who can work with him/her on schoolwork. The two students could meet after school at each other's home or talk on the telephone about schoolwork. The school guidance counselor may be able to help you find someone.

LESSON 8: "MY UNDERSTANDING OF ALCOHOL"

We should be teaching children as early as possible about the risks of drinking alcohol. Children should be made aware that some elementary school students try drinking alcohol and that this is wrong and dangerous.

There are many reasons why young people begin to drink alcohol. Helping children to explore these reasons will help them watch for situations in which they will say "No!" without hesitation. Children will also benefit by learning a collection of clear reasons for not drinking alcohol.

Activity 55: Why Some Kids Start Drinking Alcohol

Grades 3-5
Materials: One copy of the following checklist.

The following are excuses some young people give to explain why they started drinking alcohol. Although there are no good reasons for kids to drink look through these excuses with the child and check the ones that you both believe are the most common.

☐ They want to have fun.

☐ They want to feel accepted by others.

☐ They want to live dangerously.

☐ It helps them to relax.

☐ They want to forget their problems.

☐ They think it helps them socialize.

☐ There's nothing else they can think of to do.

☐ They like how it tastes.

☐ It quenches their thirst.

☐ They are curious about what will happen.

☐ Their parents drink.

☐ Their friends drink.

☐ They are trying to act like they are older.

☐ Because of commercials about alcohol.

☐ They think it will make them "cool."

☐ They are rebelling against their parents.

☐ They want to attract the opposite sex.

☐ It is inherited from their parents.

Activity 56: Reasons for Not Drinking Alcohol

Grades 3-5

Materials: One copy of the following checklist.

The following are some of the reasons why kids should not drink alcohol. Check the ones that you both believe are the best reasons.

☐ It can make you throw up.

☐ You may end up doing things that you regret.

☐ It is illegal and you may get caught.

☐ It can cause you problems at school and at home.

☐ It can result in a terrible hangover.

☐ It can keep you from having fun in other ways.

☐ Drinking too much alcohol can kill you.

☐ It can make you even more angry or very sad.

☐ It can cause you to not care about yourself.

☐ You can end up in a dangerous situation.

☐ It is addictive and can be hard to quit.

☐ Sooner or later, it can kill you.

☐ It can hurt your relationships with people in your family.

☐ You can lose respect from others your age.

☐ You can be taken advantage of in different ways.

☐ It can make you lazy.

☐ When you have a job, it can cause you to be fired.

☐ It makes you somebody that you are not.

Other Activities

Activity 57 *(Grades 2-5):* With the child, make up a skit about the negative effects of drinking alcohol. Ask a teacher if you can present your skit to their class. For example, a skit could be made showing someone falling down, becoming sick, getting into a car accident, or not being able to talk clearly. Or, develop a skit titled, "This is Your (body part) on Alcohol." Affected body parts include brain, liver, stomach, kidneys, eyes, legs, etc. Demonstrate with a prop, or with body movements, the body part affected by alcohol. If you don't have up-to-date child oriented materials on alcohol, check with a community mental health professional.

Activity 58 *(Grades 2-5):* Look through magazines and/or newspapers for advertisements of alcoholic beverages. Try to determine the strategy the advertiser is using to try to show that drinking alcohol is "cool." Cut out several of these ads and make a collage together. Discuss with the child about how these ads may encourage kids to want to drink.

Activity 59 *(Grades 2-5):* Look for a story or book on teen or pre-teen drinking. Consult your local library or school media center. Read through one of the stories or books together with the child. Stop several times during your reading of the story to discuss the situations being described.

LESSON 9: "MY UNDERSTANDING OF OTHER DRUGS"

Overall, drug abuse in youths aged 12-17 has risen by almost 80% between 1992 and 1995 according to a federal government survey.* This alarming trend indicates that new and fresh approaches are needed to discourage the use of intoxicants **before** children's first drug experience.

There are several programs available that help children learn about the dangers of drugs. Most of them present information to children in classes, books, and assembly programs. This series of activities provides a more personalized opportunity for a child to receive and discuss this kind of information about drugs within the context of a one-to-one relationship with a counselor. The following activities will provide opportunities to discuss illegal drugs, alternatives to their use, and different ways to say "No!"

*Newsweek, August 26, 1996, p. 52.

Activity 60: Who Would You Go To For Help?

Grades K-5

Materials: One copy of the following situations and list of helpers.

Read one the following situations to the child and ask, "Who would you go to for help?" Then read through the list of helpers and allow the child to select any that he/she might go to for help in that situation. Discuss others on the list that the child could also seek help from.

1. An older student shows you some pills and asks you to take one of them.

2. Some students your age start pressuring you to sniff gasoline.

3. Someone tries to get you to drink some beer.

4. Someone in your family has a drug problem.

5. A friend of yours tries to get you to smoke a cigarette.

Helpers:

- Teacher
- Principal
- Counselor
- Social Worker
- Other students
- Parents
- Police (DARE Officer)
- Nurse
- Resource Officer
- Other Person

Activity 61: "I've Heard of It"

Grades 3-5
Materials: One copy of the following checklist.

Ask the child to look over the following list and place one of the following symbols in the space before each item to indicate how familiar he/she is with the substance. Help the child learn where he/she can get more information about the dangers of any of these substances.

X = "I know a lot about it."
O = "I know a little about it."
? = "I'm not sure what this is."

☐ Marijuana

☐ Alcohol

☐ Caffeine

☐ Tobacco

☐ LSD

☐ Cocaine or Crack

☐ Angel Dust (PCP)

☐ Ecstasy

☐ Heroin

☐ 'Shrooms (psychedelic mushrooms)

☐ Speed (crystal meth)

☐ Downers (barbiturates or tranquilizers)

☐ Steroids (for body building)

☐ Inhalants (like gasoline or glue)

☐ Others (list)

_____

_____

_____

_____

Activity 62: Fun Without Drugs

Grades 3-5
Materials: One copy of the following checklist.

Some adults believe that the main reason that kids begin using drugs is because someone pushes them into it. However, the fact is that the primary reasons kids give for using alcohol, or other drugs is because they want to have fun. They decide to try drugs without actually being pushed.

For young people to make the decision to never use drugs, it is important for them to have many things they can do to have fun without being intoxicated or high. Ask the child to place a check mark in the front of each of the following things he/she would like to do to have fun without drugs.

- ☐ Play team sports such as baseball, basketball, soccer, football, or hockey.

- ☐ Play any of the above sports, without being on a formal team.

- ☐ Play games such as pool, chess, checkers, cards, video games, or board games.

- ☐ Go bowling with some friends.

- ☐ Go skating or skateboarding with friends.

- ☐ Go snow skiing or sledding with friends.

- ☐ Go swimming or boating with friends.

- ☐ Learn to play a musical instrument.

- ☐ Listen to music alone or with friends.

- ☐ Write poetry, music, and/or lyrics.

- ☐ Create something with arts or crafts.

- ☐ Get involved in one or more interest clubs.

- ☐ Take up a hobby such as collecting something.

- ☐ Take up martial arts.

- ☐ Hang out only with friends who are drug free.

- ☐ Go to the shopping mall.

- ☐ Go camping or hiking.

- ☐ Plan a trip with your friends.

- ☐ Go biking.

- ☐ Go to a local recreational facility.

- ☐ Watch television.

- ☐ Go to the movies.

- ☐ Learn to cook something special.

- ☐ Go to watch a sports team practice or play.

- ☐ Go to a park with some friends.

- ☐ Make up your own dance routine.

- ☐ Visit your local humane society and help care for the animals.

- ☐ Try out for a part in a play.

- ☐ Join a community youth group.

- ☐ Invent a game to play by yourself or with friends.

- ☐ Organize a neighborhood carnival.

- ☐ Build something with your friends.

- ☐ Go fishing.

Activity 63: A Message to a Child

Grades 3-5
Materials: None
Ask the child, "If you were going to talk with a first grader about drugs, what are three things you would say?" Have the child write his/her answers below. Then discuss them together.

1. _____

    _____

    _____

2. _____

    _____

    _____

3. _____

    _____

    _____

Other Activities

Activity 64 *(Grades K-5):* Brainstorm a list of different ways to say "No!" to someone who might offer a student a chance to use drugs. Help the child practice saying these things by role-playing different situations together.

Examples of statements include:

"No way!"   *"I've got to go!"*

"Get away from me!"   *"Never!"*

"I said 'No' and I mean 'No'!"

"Forget it!"

Activity 65 *(Grades 3-5):* Set up a time for you and the child to interview a social worker, health care worker, or the school's DARE Officer about drug problems in your community. Before the interview, decide together what questions each of you will ask.

Or, arrange to visit and interview a drug rehabilitation counselor with the child. Ask if you can have some brochures and other available information on drugs. Then, work with the child to create a presentation for younger students in the school. Note that there are several other sources for this information in your community.

Activity 66 *(Grades 3-5):* Work with the child and perhaps with others in your school to organize a drug-free celebration event in your school or community.

LESSON 10: "MY CHARACTER"

Being successful means more than merely having money, power, and other things that show your accomplishments. These things are merely signs that you have achieved some things. They do not show what kind of person you are on the inside. Character building is one way to work on your inner self. It focuses on things about you that are eventually going to be much more important in determining your success and happiness than mere symbols of success.

Counselors should work with parents, teachers, and anyone else who is attempting to help a child to grow, to help him/her realize the importance of the following "Six Pillars of Character."

1. Trustworthiness

2. Respect

3. Responsibility

4. Fairness

5. Caring

6. Citizenship

Activity 67: Learn
"The Six Pillars of Character"

Grades K-5
Materials: One copy of the "The Six Pillars of Character."

Discuss with the child one of the Six Pillars of Character. Talk together about what each word means and why it is important. You might find the following list helpful in providing examples of each Pillar. Afterwards, do something together with the child to show this type of character. Whenever you notice the child showing one of these Pillars, be sure to mention it to him/her.

The Six Pillars of Character*

1. Trustworthiness
- Be honest.
- If you find something that doesn't belong to you, return it to the owner.
- Don't cheat or steal other people's property.

2. Respect
- Be courteous and polite with others.
- Don't put other people down.
- Accept other people's differences.

3. Responsibility
- Keep your promises.
- Be reliable.
- Set a good example of behavior for others.

4. Fairness
- Be a good listener of other people's views.
- Don't take advantage of others.
- Take only your fair share.

5. Caring
- Show kindness toward others.
- Live by the Golden Rule—treat others the way you want them to treat you.
- Don't be selfish, mean, or cruel to others.

6. Citizenship
- Obey school rules.
- Obey the law.
- Be helpful to others.

*Reprinted from *Ethics: Easier Said Than Done* with permission of the Josephson Institute of Ethics ©1992

Activity 68: Trustworthiness
Grades 3-5
Materials: None

For each of the following situations, ask the child, "What did the person(s) do that was wrong?" "What could have been done differently to show better character?" "What could the person(s) do next to work things out?"

☞ Ron saw another student drop a dollar bill on the floor. He picked up the money and put it in his pocket. Later, Ron spent it on some candy.

☞ Mara told a secret to her friend about a boy that she liked. Later that afternoon, Mara found out that several other students found out about it, and they started teasing her.

☞ Todd was worried about taking a test. He knew that the student sitting next to him would probably do well on it. During the test, Todd looked at the student's paper and copied some of the answers.

Activity 69: Respect
Grades 3-5
Materials: None

Continue the same procedures with the following:

☞ A group of students were making fun of a girl because of the way she looked. John heard the other students tease her, and then started making fun of the girl too.

☞ Several students were going to Natalie's birthday party. But one girl said she couldn't come because of her religion. Natalie became angry and said to the other girls, "That's just an excuse! She just doesn't want to come."

☞ The teacher told Matt to stop talking with others and get to work. Matt kept on talking, anyway.

Activity 70: Responsibility
Grades 3-5
Materials: None

Continue the same procedures with the following:

☞   John promised his parents that he would go straight home and clean up his room after school. Instead, he went to the park with his friends.

☞   LaToya didn't complete any of her homework for the third day in a row. She told her teacher that she forgot it again.

☞   Brian borrowed a CD from a friend. While he had it, Brian lent it to another friend who lost it.

Activity 71: Fairness
Grades 3-5
Materials: None

Continue the same procedures with the following:

☞   Michael heard from other students that Jeremy stole his lunch money out of his desk. When Jeremy wasn't around, Michael reached into Jeremy's desk and took something of his.

☞   Two girls worked equally hard on a science project. Once they finished, one girl told the teacher that she had done most of the work.

☞   Darla used to be best friends with Patricia. Then Patricia started spending time with another girl. So, Darla made up a lie about the other girl and told it to several people.

Activity 72: Caring
Grades 3-5
Materials: None

Continue the same procedures with the following:

☞ A new boy in school began to cry as he sat at his desk. Some of the other students started laughing at him.

☞ Krista tried to tell Carrie that she was sorry for something she did. Carrie just looked away and kept walking without saying a word.

☞ During the winter, Carla's parents told her that they were having money problems and asked her to please keep the front door to the house closed better so that the heat wouldn't be wasted. That evening, Carla locked her bedroom door, put on her coat, and opened up her window. Then she lit up a cigarette and blew the smoke out the window.

Activity 73: Citizenship
Grades K-5
Materials: None

Continue the same procedures with the following:

☞ Jason heard that one of his friends was going to steal money from the teacher's desk. He didn't want to say anything because he didn't want to lose his friend.

☞ Mark stole a computer game from a large store. He said that the store was owned by rich people who have "plenty of money."

☞ Barbara never volunteered to help anyone unless she received something for it.

Other Activities

Activity 74 *(Grades K-5)*: Have a "Character Scavenger Hunt" with the child. Search for examples of people showing each of the Six Pillars. These examples may be found by observing other students at play during recess or at lunch. They may also be found in magazine pictures, books, or on television.

Activity 75 *(Grades K-5)*: Have the child draw or construct six large pillars holding up a paper or cardboard roof. On each pillar should be labeled the name of the character trait. Then, use this as a backdrop for mini-plays about each Pillar of Character. Have the child use small figures of people and/or animals to act out the stories.

LESSON 11:
"My Future Career"

Your career may seem like a long way off in the future. But, now is the time to begin thinking about different careers that are interesting to you.

There are many different kinds of jobs that you could do when you grow up. Some of these jobs involve working with a team of people. Other jobs involve working with machines and equipment. Some jobs include working outdoors. Other jobs take place in an office. Some jobs involve taking care of animals or people. Other jobs involve showing your art, music, or sports talents. There are many, many kinds of jobs to choose from.

Activity 76: Career Charades
Grades K-5
Materials: 10-20 index cards

Write the name of a different career on each of 10-20 index cards. Then place these cards in a bag or box and shake them up. Next, you and the child should each take a turn picking out a card and acting out the career while the other tries to guess what it is. Afterwards, take some time to discuss the child's understanding of and feelings toward the career.

Activity 77: Service Learning
Grades K-5
Materials: None

Find a service learning project in your community which you and the child can complete together. Service learning involves students in field projects that attempt to meet some community need. Examples of service learning projects include:

- Adopting a grandparent at a nursing home.
- Planting a tree, bush, or flower.
- Helping to keep an area of a park clean.
- Making a gift to send to a needy person in your community.
- Putting together a "care package" for a child from another country.
- Adopting a friend at a local children's home.
- Volunteering to care for animals at a local wildlife shelter.

When working together on a service learning project, help the child explore how the experience is good preparation for working in a career. For example, it may help him/her to learn how to be more generous, dependable, hard working, persistent, and/or committed.

Activity 78: Family Career Tree
Grades K-5
Materials: Large sheet of drawing paper or poster board, index cards, crayons or magic markers, tape or paste.

Have the child draw and/or write about the careers of different family members. If possible ask the child to interview family members and describe each on an index card. Other cards could be completed on ancestors.

Then, ask the child to draw a tree on a large sheet of drawing paper or poster board. Then, tape or paste each index card onto the tree. The child may create his/her tree following a "Family Tree" format. Or, your child could merely draw a tree and place the cards randomly in the branches.

Activity 79: Job Shadowing
Grades K-5
Materials: None

If possible, arrange with a parent or relative for the child to visit him/her in their work setting. Allow him/her to observe that person at work and become involved in a job related task, if this is possible and appropriate. In addition, you might arrange for the child to shadow workers in other careers. Or, you might work out a time for the child to meet and shadow a high school student who is currently taking classes in a vocational program.

Activity 80: Career Field Trips
Grades K-5
Materials: None

Arrange field trips for the child to visit different career settings where he/she can observe people at work. For example, visit a hospital, factory, farm, police or fire department, local government office, department store, airport, or construction project.

Activity 81: Tools of the Trade
Grades K-5
Materials: Drawing paper (4-10 sheets), crayons or magic markers

Ask the child to make a booklet filled with drawings of tools used in different careers. Each page will display the name of the career and the tools used. As an option, help the child collect some real tools and make a display for other children to learn about the careers.

Activity 82: What's Important to You?

Grades 3-5
Materials: A copy of the following list.

The following are some of the reasons why people choose and enjoy certain careers over others. Ask the child to select the three most important things he/she would like to find in a career. Then, have the child rank these three items according to what is most important to him/her. Follow-up with a discussion about what careers might be most suited to him/her.

- ☐ Working with others in a team
- ☐ Working alone
- ☐ Working outdoors
- ☐ Being my own boss
- ☐ Fixing or repairing things
- ☐ Working with computers
- ☐ Working with people or animals
- ☐ Working with numbers
- ☐ Playing a sport
- ☐ Entertaining others
- ☐ Drawing or painting
- ☐ Traveling
- ☐ Selling things
- ☐ Helping people solve their problems
- ☐ Playing a musical instrument or singing
- ☐ Building things

Other Activities

Activity 83 *(Grades K-5):* Ask the child to interview different adults at his/her school and at home. The child should ask the adults what careers they thought about when they were in elementary school. Then, what different jobs did they have before they entered the career they are in presently. Discuss with him/her how some people change careers several times during their lives.

Activity 84 *(Grades K-5):* In your community, find someone (not related to the child) who will give a monetary gift to your child for completing some brief job. Then, go with the child to interview for the job. Next, schedule a time to do the job and emphasize the importance of getting there ready and on time. Then, work together to complete the task and share the pay between you. For example, rake or clean a yard, mop a floor, sweep a porch or sidewalk, or cook a special meal for someone.

Activity 85 *(Grades K-5):* Go to the local library with the child. Together, look up books on three to five careers that interest him/her. Explore some of these books together and discuss how these careers are similar and how they are different from one another.

References

Bowman, R.P. (1987). The Test Buster Pep Rally. Minneapolis, MN: Educational Media.

Bowman, R.P. (1997). Study With a Buddy. Chapin, SC: YouthLight, Inc. (In development).

Bowman, R.P. & Chanaca, J. Jr. (1993) Peer Pals. Circle Pines, MN: American Guidance Services.

Josephson Institute of Ethics (Dec., 1992). Developing Moral Values in Youth. Ethics: Easier Said Than Done. (Marina Del Rey, CA), Issues 19&20, 80-81.